The Grass is Greener Where you Water it

Seven Steps to Becoming the Best Version of Yourself

By Constance Carter

Copyright © 2017 Constance Carter

All rights reserved.

ISBN: 9781521188798

The contents of this book may not be reproduced, duplicated or transmitted without direct written permission from the author.

Under no circumstances will any legal responsibility or blame be held against the publisher for any reparation, damages, or monetary loss due to the information herein, either directly or indirectly.

<u>Legal Notice:</u>

This book is copyright protected. This is only for personal use. You cannot amend, distribute, sell, use, quote or paraphrase any part or the content within this book without the consent of the author.

<u>Disclaimer Notice:</u>

Please note the information contained within this document is for educational and entertainment purposes only. Every attempt has been made to provide accurate, up to date and reliable complete information. No warranties of any kind are expressed or implied. Readers acknowledge that the author is not engaging in the rendering of legal, financial, medical or professional advice. The content of this book has been derived from various sources. Please consult a licensed professional before attempting any techniques outlined in this book.

By reading this document, the reader agrees that under no circumstances are is the author responsible for any losses, direct or indirect, which are incurred as a result of the use of information contained within this document, including, but not limited to, —errors, omissions, or inaccuracies.

DEDICATION

For all of our Happy Brain Followers
Know that *you are* Limitless

CONTENTS

	Introduction	Pg 1
1	Step 1 – Get off the Roundabout	Pg 3
2	Step 2 – Discover your Passions	Pg 7
3	Step 3 and 4 – Find Calm in the Storm	Pg 11
4	Step 5 and 6 – Watering the Grass in the Right places	Pg 15
5	Step 7 – Keeping the Grass Watered	Pg 20
	Conclusion	Pg 25

INTRODUCTION

First of all I just want to thank you and congratulate you on downloading this book "The Grass is Greener Where You Water it – Seven Steps to Becoming the Best Version of Yourself."

This book contains seven powerful and proven steps on how to become the best version of yourself. Implement these strategies to simplify your life for a more motivated, driven and happier you!

For the past twenty years, I have been working to help people to improve the way that they see themselves, so that they can improve their lives. This book is written from experience and from the responses of people whose lives have become dull or mundane, or who let self-esteem get in the way of being fully realized. Every day of the week, people are diagnosed with anxiety related diseases and from the look of the amount of prescriptions written – as per stats available to everyone on the Internet – something really isn't working. People still see someone else's grass as being greener. The problem is that this is not a true picture of reality.

This book aims to help those who find themselves in a rut to step beyond that and to become the very best human being they can be. The world that we live in offers so many opportunities – some of them obvious and others obscured or hidden behind a barrage of beliefs. Drop those beliefs and open yourself up to change. You will find that the seven steps within this book, representing the seven days, will change your attitude. They will also change your approach to life, which is where so many people make mistakes.

There are so many ways in which you can improve who you are, simply by watering the grass in the right places. This book helps you to do that. In fact, you may even find that your grass is greener than everyone else's. It's just a case of perspective.

1 STEP 1 – GET OFF THE ROUNDABOUT

On day one, you need to learn that the roundabout of life that you are on is your choice. That's right. It isn't something that you deserve or that you are entitled to. It is simply a choice. You may be wondering how that happens. For instance, people don't choose to be poor or rich. They don't choose to be infirm. However, the control that you have over whether you stay on the monotonous roundabout of life, or whether you embrace life to its fullest is within your control. The thoughts that come through your mind are what dictate how happy you are with what your life is or where it is going. For example, if you think in a negative manner, then the only thing you gain from that is negativity. What's making you think in a negative manner? This is where the answer lies. You need to decide what it is.

For the first day of this seven-day change program, you need to be aware of your thought processes. Have a piece of paper handy and write down what elements of your day are negative. Whenever you have a negative thought, write it down. When you feel that life isn't offering you very much, it's probably as a direct result of misguided thoughts. We all have the capacity to become depressed. We all have the capacity to become miserable, and we allow ourselves to become these things by overloading the mind with negativity. Think of it realistically. Being poor doesn't necessarily mean that people are not happy. There has to be some tangible thing or element in your life that is contributing to negativity. That thing is thought.

A thought is a fleeting moment. Whether you enlarge on that thought or not is a conscious choice. For example, I woke up this morning and the rain was pouring. Now there's two ways I can go about my day. I can either constantly look outside the window knowing what work I have to do outdoors and complain about the rain, or I can redirect my thoughts to work I have to do indoors and simply get on with something else that is positive. You have to control your thoughts and stop making negative chains out of bad events. Bad events happen to everyone, but not everyone uses that as an excuse to be miserable and unhappy.

Thus, by keeping an eye on your thoughts today and writing down the negative ones, you can then swing them around and turn them into positive events in your day. Let me show you a little bit about how to do this:

Thought: Shit, I've got a hangover.

Potential of day: Be miserable, stay in bed and feel awful.

Where the grass is greener: Get up, have a shower, drink something to help the head and choose to do things that make that hangover go away. In this case, I would suggest something outdoors or something inspiring, so that the hangover is less imposing in your life.

Thought: I really don't want to paint the house today.

Potential of day: Do the painting and be thoroughly miserable.

Where the grass is greener: If you paint while you are not in the mood to do it, you will not do it to the best of your ability. Thus, painting when forced to is pointless. You could get inventive and put your favorite radio station on to keep you company or find a job that is equally as important but that you do enjoy doing. It could be something mundane, but it may be something that needs doing nonetheless. Do it. Feel great about having achieved it.

Thought: I am fat and worthless.

Potential of day: I sit around and feel sorry for myself and overeat comfort foods because it gives me a temporary sugar high.

Where the grass is greener: I put the thought of my size and worth out of my mind and do something positive to make myself feel better about who I am.

So, for this day only, you are going to examine your negative thoughts and come up with alternatives where the grass is greener. That doesn't mean procrastination. It means finding alternative thoughts that are more geared toward success. You need to replace any negative thoughts with positive acts. Get off the self-destructive roundabout of life and stop going around in circles. It's an actual CHOICE! You have so much power in your life that you are not using. On this first day, start to use it. You will achieve. You will feel the strength of positivity and you will start to feel much happier about yourself. This is an exercise that you should carry on over the course of the next week, even though you are introducing new elements into your life to make you feel the best that you possibly can feel and thus, become a better person.

Life is only mundane if you come up with mundane solutions to everyday problems. Instead of doing that, think of the problem and then write down the potential solutions. Recognize the solution that is negative and try to come up with solutions that make the grass greener. You can do it, and when you start to do this instead of allowing negativity to hit home, you start living your life in a much different way.

Jon was always a pessimist. He saw the dark side of every situation, until one day, he decided that the roundabout of life was getting to him. He observed people and that observation helped him to see that other people managed to live their lives quite happily without always seeing the negative side of everything. He also read many books that explained about the difference between the cup half full and the cup half empty.

He had to admit that he had lived his life by the cup half empty rules and decided that it was time to change that. Making a mental effort to overcome problems, he wrote down what his problems were. Then he decided to label his answers to the problems in two ways. One was the pessimistic approach that he knew he was always guilty of and the other was by using intuition – a gift that all of us have but that few of us use. We call this the "Green grass solution."

When you write down your problem and try to analyze it from these different perspectives, you begin to see the choices that are open to you. Just like Mike did, you will be able to see how obvious happiness is when you look for it in your answers to problems posed by life:

Problem: My car is dirty.

Solution with cup half empty – I will do it one day.

Gut instinct or green grass solution – Get out a bucket and lots of soapy water when the sun is shining.

Result – the car lasts longer. You feel good about it; the car looks great and you get a suntan in the meanwhile!

It is up to you to find creative solutions. Be inventive and use your intuitive processes. You already know what the right answers are. Most people don't. They just go through life taking mediocre choices because they see them as the easy way out, when in fact, it is the mediocre nature of their choices that make the people who act on them mediocre as well. Fight mediocrity. If you want to be the best person you can be, you need to step beyond the mediocre and out of your comfort zone to find that balance that says you are the best you can be. Once you do, you can get off the roundabout that seems to make your life miserable and step up when needs must, to put your life back on track again.

2 STEP 2 – DISCOVER YOUR PASSIONS

Passions are drivers. They are feelings you have inside of you that make you do things to the best of your ability. You may have a passion for art and when you paint, you give your best to the picture that you are painting. You may have a passion for photography and take wonderful pictures, because you are driven by your desire to improve the scope of the photographs that you take. Everyone has passions. For example, I have a passion for writing poetry. I also have a passion for having a nice home. Passions are things we do without any effort. They are things that we love to have in our lives. Try and write down what you believe your passions are. Here is a potential list, however, make sure you are totally honest about what your passions are:

I love dancing

I love yoga

I love having a clean car

I love gardening

I love organization

I love chaos

The last two on this list were put there intentionally because these are passions that may be held by entrepreneurs to help drive them to do better things. Organization helps people to become more productive and people who embrace organization may be unhappy when things are not organized. You should be able to tell the difference between a passion and an obsession. Being obsessively anything is bad for your mind because it works overtime trying to achieve that perfection that is often not possible. Some people say that they love and thrive on chaos, and it's true to a certain extent, though if you are someone who believes in the chaos theory, you need to work out whether you love chaos and feel passionately about it, or whether your life is chaotic because you haven't actually achieved any kind of organization in your life.

Popular entrepreneur, Richard Branson, keeps a notebook with him at all times. He is a very enthused and passionate person whose business is driven by that passion, but he acknowledges that when you have ideas, you do need to note them down so that you can follow them through when time permits. His passion is his business. Close your eyes for a moment and write down the things you feel passionate about because these are the things that drive you forward in your life and help to make you feel successful. If you can't find any passion that's currently in your life, then sometimes you need to look back over your life and try and find times when you were at your happiest. Perhaps you have moved on, but instead of choosing greener grass, you moved on to barren pasture.

Kevin moved on in his career. He was in a better paid job. He had a more expensive home and could supply his family with everything material they had ever wanted. When he tried to find the passion within his life, however, he found that it was decidedly lacking. He hated his job. He came home miserable because of it. His wife was being exceedingly difficult and his children didn't really relate to him because he was never there when they needed him to be. What Kevin found when he looked back through his life was that his passion was at its highest level when he was a student and learning new things. That element was missing from his life. He worked long hours in a job he despised for people he didn't even like, and all the passion had been driven out of his life by his choice of job and lifestyle.

You may say that you can't step back to a time when you were passionate, but you can, and although it's not the easiest of things to do, you can work toward being a person that you believe in, instead of bending the shape of that person to suit what other people demand of you. Kevin sat down and talked to his family about his feelings.

They were unaware that he was so unhappy. When they finally came to an agreement on where their lives would take them from now on, they found solutions. Kevin was able to put his passions back into his life and became a better person. His wife got more from the relationship as well, and the kids found that spending time with their father broke that barrier that had been placed between them by the work that he did. He made changes that were huge changes, downsizing the home, packing in his job, taking up a new career that he would be able to share with his wife and working from home.

You can't do all that in a day. What you can do is work out what your passions are because these are things that will drive you. In Kevin's case, he had always assumed that he liked gardening because it got him away from a nagging wife. In fact, the nagging wife wasn't the problem. The job was. Gardening was his escape into something he felt passionately about. By combining his passion with his work, he started his own business as a landscaper with his wife doing the administrative work that bored him. She had a passion for organization. Today, your step of the day is to find your passion.

What drives you in life all the time are your passions. These give you the biggest buzz you can expect out of life. If you can align these with your work and your home life, then you will find that your incentive improves and that the grass actually starts to become greener.

There's another reason why your passions drive you so much. You ENJOY them and they make you happy. A happy person is always going to be a better person than one who is compromising on happiness to survive. You need to find a way to balance your life so that your passions become part of your everyday life.

Jim worked away from home on the oil rigs. He had to do the job because the money he earned allowed them to live in the cottage of their dreams. However, the job wasn't his dream job. Going to work away from home made him sad so he had to look for something that put happiness back into the picture to compensate for that sadness. You can't be the best person possible if part of you is drowning in sadness. There was no chance that he could give up his job because it was a means to an end, but what he decided he could do was use part of what he earned to finance one of his passions – which was to make musical instruments.

In his workshop at home, he set himself up so that he could work on marquetry and produce instruments that were wonderful, and that would be appreciated by people who loved music. Eventually, he was able to turn this passion into an earning potential, and when he did that, he was able to cut down on the number of hours spent away from home. So enthused was he by his passion that it took several years to get to that stage, but he is now in a stage of his life where he believes perfect happiness exists. Yes, he admits, you need obligation of some kind, but you also need the drive of passion to fire up your enthusiasm and to make whatever success you want in your life happen.

Write down what you feel passionately about and then write down how you can entertain this kind of passion within your life. The best way of doing this is to figure out your 'why'. Why are you passionate about something? To become the best person you can be, you need passion and drive, and you also need it not to come too easily. You need to put in the hard work so that your journey becomes a very worthwhile one.

Perhaps you can't have everything that you want straight away. Jim couldn't. He had to set himself up, he had to learn and he had to work very hard indeed to achieve the kind of level of success he managed to achieve. The thing that drove him toward it was his passion and belief in his own abilities. That's what you need to find because once you do, you will become better able to do whatever your dreams dictate and still live a relatively affluent lifestyle.

Your dreams may be a long way away from fruition, but if they are penned down on paper and you know what they are, at least you know your direction and are able to head in that direction. People who do not recognize their passions can never be the best people possible in their lives because there's a missing element, and one that is vital to that achievement of self-realization.

This takes time, so start now. You will be thanking yourself in three months, one year, three years' time

3 STEP 3 AND 4 – FIND CALM IN THE STORM

Everyone needs three elements in their lives. They need good health, they need good food and they need plenty of rest. The human body was designed in such a way that these three elements are essential to life. However, with everyone scrambling to be better than everyone else in this consumer society, something has gone terribly wrong. People are placing importance in all the wrong things. The size of the TV has become more important than whether you sit down for a meal. The make and model of the car has become more important than how much time you spend at leisure with your family. Having the latest iPhone has become more important than spending a little money on a family outing. Society today skews everything in favor of consumerism. Thus, people equate earning money with happiness. If you haven't got money, how can you buy the latest iPhone? What they don't see is how much they are letting material possessions ruin their lives. Minimalists have the right idea, and more and more people are jumping onto the RV lifestyle, where both of these types of choice involve cutting back on things that are unnecessary. Let's face it, there wouldn't be much point in crowding an RV with all the gadgets one finds in the home because there would be very little room to move. Similarly, minimalists have made choices and the biggest choice they make is in deciding that there is more to be gained from owning less.

The trouble with the lifestyle that we have today is that we urge people, starting with kids, toward being successful, and the word "successful" has been misinterpreted to such an extent that humans believe the only way to find any semblance of happiness is to own things. It isn't. Amid all this confusion, people work longer hours to gain the money they need to finance these ideas and ideals. A bigger house, a bigger car all demand more earnings, and more earnings means putting in more time. No wonder people are suffering from anxiety. The self-inflicted search for an elusive success isn't giving them the rewards that they thought it would. Thus, changes are needed.

Step 3 – Day 3 – Declutter the home

You need to decide all the things that are not important to you. They may be clouding your judgement. For example, do you really need all those items you have in the closet? While you hold onto old clothing that no longer fits, you remind yourself of your failure. As you take each item out of the closet, decide whether it's an item that gives you joy. It if doesn't you have three choices. Bin it, place it in a bag for charity or put it into a bag for sale at a garage sale. The grass isn't green because it doesn't have room to grow. Let the grass grow and have space to grow. When you whittle down your possessions, your home becomes much more comfortable to live in and your life becomes more manageable. Having less means tidying and cleaning less which frees your time for things of more value such as spending time with family or friends or following your passions. Less is more and this will assist you with Step 4.

If you need to plan the decluttering process, do it. Remember, it's taken you years to get to this stage where your life is filled with material things. It's a good idea to set aside a week for yourself and to work toward having the whole house decluttered by the end of that week. In fact, I could make it easier for you. Use the first days – while you have plenty of energy – to do the most difficult rooms in the house. You may even find that you have time at the end of the week to add a touch of paint or to make real changes to your home that will make you feel happier and less obligated.

Step 4 – Day 4 Clear the cluttered mind

If you have never meditated before, it's probably about time you tried. If you feel that you need help with a step like this, you can enroll with a yoga class and get advice from experienced members and the teacher. If, however, you have the necessary willpower to keep to your meditation practice daily, then go for it. Sit in a seat that is comfortable. You don't have to take the lotus position. Make sure your body is well supported and that your back is straight. Make sure your feet are planted on the ground and hold one hand on your lap palm upward and then place the other hand into it, the same way up. Touch thumbs.

The atmosphere for meditation when you are new to it should be quiet. You should have a good passage of air and make sure that noises from outside are minimal. Close your eyes to take away even more distraction. You will need to do this for about 20 minutes a day. Now, breathe in through the nostrils and feel the air going deep into your gut. Hold the breath for a moment and breathe out. You won't be accustomed to breathing this deeply but you will need to practice.

- Breathe in to the count of eight
- Hold the breath for a few seconds

- Breathe out to the count of ten

This whole procedure counts as one. Repeat it and count two and so on until you reach ten.

So, where's the trick? The trick is in what you think about while you are meditating. You are supposed to confine your thoughts to the breathing process and the counting, although once you are more experienced at meditation, you will be able to do this without actually having to use the numbers in your head. You will feel the energy going into your body. You will feel it stay there for a moment, and you will feel it leave.

If you think of other things – and believe me everyone does – you simply acknowledge the thought, dismiss it and let it go and go back to the beginning again with the breathing process shown above and counting one. You are not a failure if you cannot concentrate sufficiently for it to make a difference in the early stages. Everyone is the same. You have to recognize that like material possessions, less is more and that applies to thoughts too.

After the decluttering process

When your mind and your home are uncluttered, make room in your life for nature. Go to a place where you are inspired. I find that the best kind of places to help your inspirational levels are beaches or natural environments that allow you to see for miles, and the best time of day is sunset or sunrise. If you live by a beach, this is ideal. The reason those times are chosen is because you can see the world without everything cluttering what you see. Clutter messes up the mind. Imagine a beach that is empty and a sunset in the background. Now imagine a beach filled with screaming kids and confusion and you can see how decluttering works in a physical sense. The beach at sunset is going to fill your mind with inspiration. I feel so humble when I encounter a scene such as a sunset or sunrise on my own. I am surrounded by the beauty of the earth that was created many years ago, and that has all the elements that make me feel small in comparison.

When you declutter your thinking space, such as visiting a place like this, you fill your mind with awe and you are able to feel the spiritual side of your personality kick in. I know, in comparison with what I see, that I am small and insignificant. However, I also know that small things make up a part of the world, and that the grains of sand on the beach have their place – regardless of their smallness. Thus, I have a place too, but I need to put aside any sense of superiority. I need to put away thoughts that are worldly and sometimes clutter my thought processes and see beyond those things that may have brought my mind into the realms of dissatisfaction. Often, our worries are our worst enemies and spirituality helps you to proportion things in a better way, so that you see the bigger picture, rather than the small one.

4 STEP 5 AND 6 – WATERING THE GRASS IN THE RIGHT PLACES

When the grass is greener in one patch than it is in another, it's because the area that isn't green wasn't watered. We chose this title on purpose because people can easily relate to it. The areas of your life that are complex and unsatisfactory are like that because you haven't done much to make them different. For example, you let the weeds grow. Let's take a look at the steps you can take to clean up these areas so that you maximize your own potential.

Step 5 – Day 5 – Work out which friends add to your life

Often, people are held back because of the choices they make in their friendships. For example, if you are surrounded by people who are negative toward you, you begin to feel bad about yourself. It's a little like the grass being drowned out with weeds. You need to sort out which of your friends are weeds and which are blades of grass that can be nurtured. So how do you do that? Make a list of everyone that you know, or go through your phone book, and then split them into categories. Good friends where no questions need to be asked can be labeled with the name "Good friends." These are people who are always there when you need them but there will also be a little give and take on occasions. People who you dread seeing will be the next set. These may be people who use you, those who are always a negative influence and those who are really not welcome in your life. These are the people you have to learn to say "no" to.

All grass needs fertilizer. In the case of friendships, the feed that helps make the grass greener are those friendships that are long term and part of your roots. If you have friends that you haven't contacted for a while but feel guilty about neglecting, mark these as priorities. These are people who matter and you need to make amends. In this case, telephone each of the neglected friends and make the phone call all about catching up with their news rather than centering upon your news. It's not about you. It's about them. Of course, you should answer questions your friends may have, but try to be upbeat and friendly because you are not using these people to pass negativity to.

Step 6 – Day 6 – Be with People who like you for who you are

We all have quirks. One of my best friends enjoys the fact that I can still cartwheel at my age and doesn't mind the fact that I quite happily eat porridge for supper. Friends who are worth their weight in gold are those who love you for the person that you are. Drop the users. Drop the people who make you feel bad about yourself and change the list regularly because you need to be surrounded by people who approve of you. You also need to approve of them. What you are doing is reinforcing who you are and playing on your own strengths. A friend of mine used to avoid me because she felt that I was so much more successful than she was. It was a mistake. When we actually got together, we still had all the same things in common that we always had.

Be proud of who you are, but not so proud that you put people off. If you want to be outrageous on occasion, you can be, but try not to embarrass people too much. When you are unhappy in your life and see all those brown patches in the lawn, you need to mend them one by one and then fertilize them to ensure that they stay green. If you alienate people by being negative, it's likely that you will see those patches of brown appearing and sometimes, all it takes is a little effort on your part to make things right again.

I counsel a lot of people and one of the most stubborn habits that unhappy people have is being afraid to say "sorry", or being so stubborn that they wait for someone else to say "sorry." You could be waiting a lifetime and causing yourself and others a lot of unhappiness. What does it matter who apologizes? Stop being stubborn and apologize if you find that there is friction between you and a good friend. It really does take two to argue, but it only takes one to say "sorry" and mend awkward situations.

All the steps in this chapter have been about friendships. This can include colleagues, people who have married into your family, family members and people you have known all your life. These can be considered as the blades of grass. The weeds are those people who take something away from your happiness. Let go of these and leave more space for those who appreciate you and you automatically make your life a better place to be as well as making the grass very green indeed on your side of the fence. If you find ailing blades of grass or people you can help along the way, do so. It makes you a better person and it spreads happiness as well. When you manage to do that, you increase the size of the grass field that makes up your life and it stays green because you care enough to water it in all the right places. Nurture new friendships and keep those that are of value to you alive and kicking because these will help to make you the complete person that you are.

5 STEP 7 – KEEPING THE GRASS WATERED

In the height of summer, people are busy with their own lives. You have to take this step if you really want to water the grass and keep it green:

Step 7 – Day 7 – Appreciate everything and everyone you allow into your life

We often forget people and get wrapped up in our own existence to the extent that we don't let people in. You do need to. When someone offers to listen, don't be so proud. Let them listen. What you do is make up the building blocks in a relationship, and provided you are not always needy and give nothing in return, what you do by letting others into your life is open your heart to receive them.

Meet new people and make sure that you always keep your heart open to listening. Sometimes you find solutions to your own problems from listening to others. You have to decide whether these are people you want to keep in your life but positive people are all around, and it will be these people who help you to get back on your feet after you have experienced setbacks.

Eleanor was a 56-year-old widow. She was hurt by the death of her husband and found herself becoming more and more reclusive. It wasn't because people didn't care. It was because she alienated everyone who tried to become her friend or be a friend in need. Little by little her life became a very lonely place – one where you could imagine the grass to be dead or so badly neglected that it lost its greenness. Eventually, following a breakdown, she met people whose lives were equally lonely in the hospital where she was treated for her depression. Ten years on, she has learned that bad things happen, but that there are seasons in life and the cycle of life continues regardless of changes. She now runs a club for people who are bereaved and recognizes all the symptoms of giving up on life.

If you want to see the grass green, then you have to sometimes realize that others are experiencing bad times as well. Nurture those friendships and water the grass. Serve up a cup of tea to an old lady who lives alone and bake her a cake. Each little bit of sunshine that you put into someone else's life helps your heart to become strong and healthy. Be there for people and make sure that you are there to mop up the tears and mend things. In this very moment in your life, you have a choice. Make a difference or let the grass grow uneven and brown. On this last day of your seven days, it's important to go over all the lessons that you have learned over the previous week. Remember, grass continues to grow and needs all the same kind of attention to keep it looking healthy.

If you ever feel a lack of inspiration or find that you are feeling a bit overwhelmed by life, there is nothing better than a reality check. One of the best ways that I know how is to get up close and personal with nature. If you have a beauty spot near where you live, then visit it at either sunset or sunrise and see how big the world looks and how wonderful nature seems in comparison with the small things that are building up in your life. Remember, if you want nice grass, the last thing that you need is mole hills. When you allow problems to build up in your life, that's what you create. Thus, getting close to nature will help you to put everything back into perspective.

You can look upon the scene and realize how small and unimportant all the worldly problems are that you have surrounded yourself with. You actually gain something else as well when you take this opportunity to let the world shine on you. You gain something called humility.

Humility is a wonderful tool. It's a little like plant food for the lawn. It makes the lawn grow stronger and overcome all the obstacles that the world creates. That's a valuable lesson to learn. Humility teaches you the smallness of self and makes you reach beyond that to a place where hope resides. Look at its splendor and tell me you didn't feel that rush of hope in your heart. It is also good for the soul because it strengthens you from the inside out.

The spiritual part of your nature resides deep inside you. It's nothing to do with religion. It can be, of course, but it isn't necessarily. Spirituality is being at one with the world and a higher power than yourself, and that's a powerful help again all the bad things that can happen in the world. Perhaps this belief in a power stronger than you gives you somewhere to aim your prayers. Perhaps it just lets you know that someone is watching over you and that's equally as important. Best of all, nature teaches you the lesson that all things go in cycles, and that indeed, what may seem very barren and bare now, could actually look wonderful given a good night's sleep and a fresh look.

The snow of winter is a little like the cloak that you put over your feelings and emotions. When the snow disappears, the lawn looks like a wonderfully bright shade of green because it's had the nourishment of the water left from the snow. What you need to do is clear out the cobwebs of your life instead of hiding them under that cloak of snow. When you manage to do that, you'll be able to sort out the problems that seem huge in the cold of winter.

Throughout this book, we have used "green grass" as the example of what you should be looking at in your life. The trouble is that people go through their lives believing the grass is greener elsewhere. Imagine this case scenario.

Joseph believes his neighbors have everything he ever wanted. He is upset to the point where he needs to get away from the constant reminder of his own failure, so he moves to another town.

In that town, he finds that people are very similar to those he found in his old town. He has people around him whose grass is greener than his. No matter where Joseph tries to escape to, the story will be the same. Why? The fact is that you cannot run away from yourself. You take yourself with you, and Joseph's problem was not that the neighbor's grass was greener, it was that he had done nothing to improve the state of his grass. When he started to change who he was and how he related to people, he found the answers lay in his own approach to life, rather than his view of life through other people.

You need to be happy with who you are. You need to make yourself the very best person that you can be. Comparing yourself with others is not the way to find that perfect you. The way you find it is to go through all the steps in the chapters of this book and then look how green the grass is.

CONCLUSION

I really hope that I have been able to help you in your search for greener pastures and happiness. It's not a question of how much you water the grass. It's more a question of where you water it. If you go back through the book and take all the steps shown, you will find that your life will become a better place to be. It will take time. Seven days is all you need to find the solutions, but to put them into practice in your everyday life may take a little longer. However, it will be worth that effort. All the habits and attitudes you have in your mind now have taken you a lifetime to get there. Don't expect yourself to change overnight. All you can do is to keep the grass watered and fix those areas where the grass needs a little more loving attention.

As you go through life, you come across all kinds of people. Some will be deserving of your time, while others will be less open to your input. That's okay too, because you have to give people around you the freedom of choice and not lay your ideas at their doorsteps. When you stop expecting so much from people around you, sometimes they can astound you. In my life, I have learned that what I may have been expecting was blind-sighted, and that perhaps I was looking in the wrong direction. The change needed to come from me, rather than others. When I did manage to embrace change, life became better and I became a better human being because I was prepared to make those changes.

You are offered opportunities every day of your life to improve who you are. Take those opportunities and grasp them with both hands because regret is what makes the grass go that horrid shade of brown. If you need to apologize to people, never be too proud to do that. If you want the grass to stay green on your side of the fence, then you have to help other people as well as yourself. Your reactions to others sometimes dictate the state of your mind. Your unkindness comes back to you and makes you feel unhappy. Once you understand this, you'll be able to nurture the grass on your side of the fence and make it greener, but the best thing of all is that you can look out onto the gardens of people you love and trust and see little patches of hope that you put there, simply because you knew where their grass needed a little watering.

I hope you enjoyed this book and that you will be able to practice and experience the benefits of following through with the seven steps. Remember, you are here to be the best you can be. You are limitless so take action!

Please share your experience here at Amazon.com: https://www.amazon.com/Be-Your-Best-Becoming-Transformation-ebook/dp/B072BDT4K2

ABOUT THE AUTHOR

Constance Carter was born in South Africa and grew up in Reading, England, where she attended University to attain her degree in Physical Science.

Since then, Constance has worked as a personal trainer and yoga instructor. She currently works as a life coach and lives in Reading with her husband and their daughter.

Constance is an enthusiastic admirer of motivational speakers and follows many of them on YouTube. And it was this interest, combined with a love of writing, entrepreneurship, and for self-help, which led her to write her first book, **The Grass is Greener where you Water it – Seven Steps to Becoming the Best Version of Yourself** The book is currently available through Amazon and inside Constance provides Seven proven methods to assist anyone on realizing their potential.

When she has time to relax, Constance writes for The Happy Brain Blog. She is a lover of all things travel and adventure related.

In the future, Constance hopes to continue to help others realize their full potential, overcome their fears and just generally be brilliant!

You can contact Constance Carter at

www.thehappybrain.blog

Instagram: the_happy_brain_blog

Made in the USA
Monee, IL
20 February 2024